Rookie biographies®

Anne Frank

By Wil Mara

Reading Consultant
Cecilia Minden-Cupp, PhD
Former Director of the Language and Literacy Program
Harvard Graduate School of Education
Cambridge, Massachusetts

Children's Press®
A Division of Scholastic Inc.
New York Toronto London Auckland Sydney
Mexico City New Delhi Hong Kong
Danbury, Connecticut

Designer: Herman Adler Design
Photo Researcher: Caroline Anderson
The photo on the cover shows Anne Frank.

Library of Congress Cataloging-in-Publication Data

Mara, Wil.
 Anne Frank / By Wil Mara.
   p. cm. — (Rookie biographies)
 Includes index.
 ISBN-10: 0-516-29841-0 (lib. bdg.)   0-516-27301-9 (pbk.)
 ISBN-13: 978-0-516-29841-2 (lib. bdg.)   978-0-516-27301-3 (pbk.)
 1. Frank, Anne, 1929–1945—Juvenile literature. 2. Jewish children in the
Holocaust—Netherlands—Amsterdam—Juvenile literature. 3. Jews—Netherlands—
Amsterdam—Biography—Juvenile literature. 4. Holocaust, Jewish (1939–1945)—
Netherlands—Amsterdam—Juvenile literature. I. Title. II. Series: Rookie biography.
 DS135.N6F73486 2006
 940.53'18092—dc22   2005030097

CHILDREN'S PRESS, and ROOKIE BIOGRAPHIES®, and associated
logos are trademarks and/or registered trademarks of Scholastic Library
Publishing. SCHOLASTIC and associated logos are trademarks and/or
registered trademarks of Scholastic Inc.

1 2 3 4 5 6 7 8 9 10 R 16 15 14 13 12 11 10 09 08 07

Can you change the world by simply writing down your thoughts? Anne Frank did.

Anne (left) and her sister Margot in 1933

Anne was born in Germany on June 12, 1929. She was a happy young girl.

Anne had one older sister named Margot. The Franks were Jewish.

A political group called the Nazis (NAHT-seez) controlled Germany while Anne was growing up.

The Nazis hated people who were Jewish. They made fun of the Jews and told them where to live and what to do.

Adolf Hitler (center) led the Nazis.

Anne (second from right) and her family in Amsterdam

Anne and her family moved to the Netherlands in 1933 to escape the Nazis. The Franks hoped they would be safe in a city called Amsterdam. But the Nazis took control of the Netherlands in 1940.

The Franks went into hiding from the Nazis in Amsterdam in 1942. They hid in secret rooms above an office where Anne's father had once worked.

The office building in Amsterdam where Anne's father once worked

A bookshelf was used to hide the entrance to the secret rooms where the Franks lived.

It was hard living in these secret rooms. There was very little space.

Other Jews also hid with the Franks. Everyone had to be very quiet. The Nazis would arrest the Franks if they found out they were hiding.

Anne did her best to stay happy and hopeful. She tried to keep busy by writing in a diary.

A diary is a book of blank pages where you can write your private thoughts.

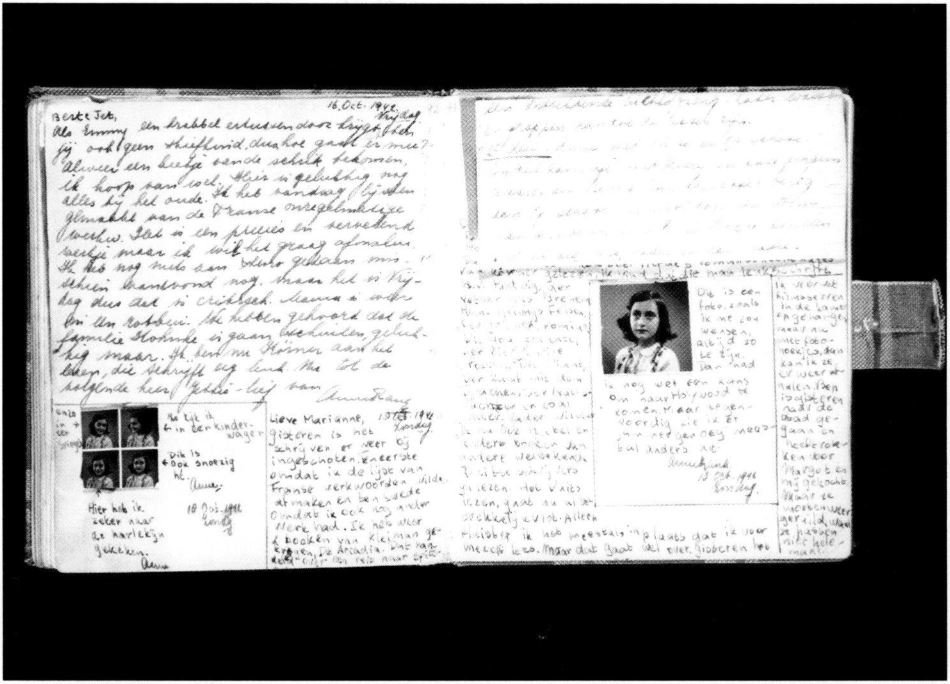

Anne's diary

Anne was very afraid of the Nazis (above). Many other Jews in Europe went into hiding because they were also afraid.

Anne wrote in her diary about how much she wanted to play outside and see the sun. She also wrote about how much she feared the Nazis.

Anne sometimes wrote about
a boy named Peter van Pels.
Peter and his family were hiding
with the Franks. Anne liked
Peter very much.

The Nazi concentration camp where Anne was sent

The Nazis found out about the Franks' secret hiding place in 1944. They sent everyone to a terrible place called a concentration camp.

Concentration camps were like prisons. The Nazis treated people in concentration camps very badly.

Anne had to do hard work
much of the day. She had little
food, and the room she slept
in at night was very cold.

Some people in concentration
camps caught illnesses and died.
The Nazis killed many others.

A prisoner in a Nazi concentration camp

These Jewish prisoners were freed from a concentration camp in 1945.

Anne became sick and died in 1945. She was only fifteen years old.

Soldiers from other countries defeated the Nazis that same year. These troops freed prisoners in the concentration camps. But many people in the camps had already died.

Peter van Pels and Anne's mother and sister all died in concentration camps. Anne's father survived. He worked to have Anne's diary published in 1947.

Anne's father, Otto Frank

28

Millions of people have read *The Diary of Anne Frank*. Anne's words show the terrible things the Nazis did. But they also tell people not to give up hope even when horrible things are happening to them.

Words You Know

Anne Frank

concentration camp

diary

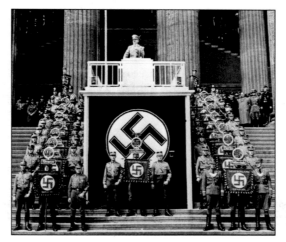

Nazis

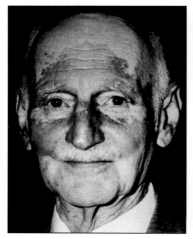

Otto Frank

Peter van Pels

Index

Amsterdam, 9, 10

birth, 5

concentration camps, 21–22, 25

death, 25

diary, 14, 17, 26, 29

The Diary of Anne Frank, 29

father, 9, 10, 13, 21, 26

Frank, Margot (sister), 5, 9, 10, 13, 21, 26

Germany, 5, 6

illnesses, 22

Jews, 5, 6, 13

mother, 9, 10, 13, 21, 26

Nazis, 6, 9, 10, 13, 17, 21, 22, 25, 29

Netherlands, 9–10

Pels, Peter van, 18, 26

secret rooms, 10, 13, 21

sister, 5, 9, 10, 13, 21, 26

About the Author

Wil Mara is the author of more than seventy-five books. He has written fiction and nonfiction for both children and adults.

Photo Credits

Photographs © 2007: akg-Images, London: 12 (Michael Teller), 28; Corbis Images/Bettmann: cover, 7, 27, 31 bottom left, 31 top center; Getty Images/Hulton Archive: 15, 30 bottom center (Anne Frank House); 3, 4, 8, 19, 30 top left, 31 bottom right (Anne Frank Fonds); The Art Archive/Picture Desk/Stapleton Collection: 16; The Image Works: 11 (Roger-Viollet), 23 (Roger-Viollet/Topham), 20, 24, 30 top right (Topham).